MW01633165

Rookie Detective
A Mystery Adventure Chapter Book for Kids

Written by Mateo Sommer

Illustrations by Henrique C. Rampazzo

Production management by Magdalene Ward

For information address LittleBigPage, 312 W. 2nd St #1934
Casper, WY 82601, United States.

Paperback ISBN: 9788367973250

First Edition

ROOKIE DETECTIVE

Mateo Sommer

You can **download** the free **audiobook** version of this **book**.

Go to the last **page** for more information!

Contents

Mom
Dad
Cassandra
Sebastian

The Major
The Cuthbertsons

Chapter One

Sebastian was late. He wanted to leave the house immediately, calling a cheery goodbye as he went, but Mom wouldn't like that. Instead, he stuck his head through the living room door.

She was watching the news. A pretty news anchor with very white teeth was saying, "—missing heiress has not been seen for years apart from rumors of questionable sightings. The search continues—"

Sebastian didn't hear the rest because Mom turned to him, muting the sound.

"What's up?" she asked.

"I'm going to the park," he said. "To join the guys in a game of baseball." He had practiced saying that in his bedroom mirror all morning. He wanted to sound casual as if meeting the guys at the park was something he did all the time.

"Oh!" Mom was surprised. She sat up to face Sebastian, moving Cassandra, his younger sister, from where she was sprawled out on Mom's lap.

"Hey!" Cassandra whined, but she also turned to Sebastian.

His eyes lingered on the television screen for a second. A photograph of a sweet-faced young woman was being shown. Another photo was placed next to it with aging software applied. As Sebastian watched, she aged, her face creasing into wrinkles. A name and phone number appeared underneath the photos.

"Can I come with you?" Cassandra asked.

Sebastian didn't really want her to tag along, but he didn't know how to say no. "Sure, I guess," he muttered.

All the way to the park, his shoulders were slumped with embarrassment that he was stuck with his little sister. He sat near the field and watched as the joyful boys divided themselves into two teams and started to play. One of the boys who was in position in the outfield caught a nearby Sebastian staring at him.

"Hey," Sebastian said glumly. "I wouldn't mind playing. Is there room for me?" He blushed pink, aware that he sounded like a bit of a loser.

The boy laughed and looked away for a moment to make sure the ball didn't need his attention. Then he looked back at Sebastian with a face full of mischief and asked, "But who will babysit her?" A few of the other boys overheard and laughed too as they looked from Sebastian to Cassandra. She stood and stuck out her tongue at the boys, about to say something to them.

"Don't!" Sebastian said, going even pinker with embarrassment. "Let's just go."

Cassandra was still twisting to glare at the boys as Sebastian dragged her toward the gate. He focused on keeping her moving and didn't see the people walking in their direction. He accidentally bumped into them and instantly recognized the pair as a new family that had recently moved to the neighborhood.

"Oh, sorry!" Sebastian said, blushing. "I didn't mean to . . ."

Cassandra twisted her wrist free from his grip while he spoke.

"Be more careful!" the woman hissed.

"Idiot!" her companion said as he glared at Sebastian.

"It was an accident, Mrs. Cuthbertson!" Cassandra loudly announced. "And he said sorry!" Mrs. Cuthbertson glared at the little girl.

Sebastian, now completely red-faced, grabbed Cassandra's hand again and stepped around the couple. But he could still hear them.

"Little idiots."

"Twerps!" Mr. Cuthbertson agreed.

They both laughed meanly.

At the same time, three boys on the baseball diamond burst out laughing too. Sebastian's ears burned a fiery red. He wasn't sure if they had heard the Cuthbertson's comments, but it felt like everyone in the world was laughing at him.

Cassandra stopped walking and her mouth fell open. Sebastian knew that she was about to argue again.

"Leave it alone!" he whispered, tugging her out through the park gate.

"Why did you stop me?" she asked. "They were really mean!"

He didn't answer and just walked home as fast as he could. Sebastian experienced a mixture of emotions. He felt hot and small, as though he was about to cry.

"Hello!" Mom greeted, as they entered the house. "You were only gone fifteen minutes! What happened?"

"The guys didn't want to play ball with me because of Cassandra," Sebastian said, knowing he was being mean. "They said I was too busy babysitting. I wish she hadn't come."

Cassandra's mouth opened again, and this time there was no stopping her.

"No!" she exclaimed. "They didn't want you to play because you're a big chicken who never speaks up! If you didn't want me to come, all you needed to say was, 'No, Cassandra.' I would've stayed home with Mom and watched TV!"

Sebastian stared at the carpet in front of him. He knew she was right. She had never been a sulky child and would have accepted his "no" with ease. He was being unfair, but he didn't know how to make it up to her.

"Sebastian?" Mom's voice was gentle but firm. "I think you owe your sister an apology."

He shrugged, still staring at the carpet. His eyes followed the swirling pattern. Then he muttered, "I'm going to talk to Dad. *He* understands me."

Mom took a deep breath, but he turned and hurried away before she could insist that he apologize. He was desperate to talk to his dad about how everything had gone wrong. Dad was good at talking things through and pointing out what Sebastian could have done differently. He could also make Sebastian feel better when he felt bad, like now.

Chapter Two

Sebastian moved quickly to Dad's home office. The door was closed, but it was never locked, and it swung open at his touch. He loved the office. Dad was a successful private detective, and Mom was incredibly proud of him. She had decorated the space with gifts his grateful clients had sent. She also hung framed newspaper articles about cases he'd solved: the Oaktree Jewel Heist; the Case of the Principal's Dummy; and the Missing Millions. She'd also found a tailor's mannequin to dress up with the disguises he used on jobs. Currently, it wore a curly blond wig, thick-framed glasses, and a bright purple coat.

Dad had explained to the children that people seeing him in disguise would remember the obvious things. Therefore, as soon as he took them off again, they wouldn't recognize him. Cassandra had clapped her hands happily as they'd watched him transform from one person into another. When he'd finally returned to being just Dad, Sebastian had been almost breathless with admiration. But he never said anything, always unsure of sounding silly. But Dad somehow always knew. Dad *got* Sebastian in a way that no one else did. He was certain Dad would make him feel better about the terrible afternoon.

But Dad wasn't there.

Sebastian ran a finger along the back of a cat ornament a client had given Dad when he'd found her missing Persian kitten. The office was tidy, everything arranged neatly, the chair tucked in. Dad obviously hadn't been there for a while. In fact . . . Sebastian frowned. He hadn't seen Dad at all today!

Mom came into the office behind him. "Dad's not here," she said. "He thought he'd be home for lunch, but he wasn't. He hasn't called either." Her tone sounded tight, as though she was upset with Sebastian. Maybe because he had left the room without apologizing to Cassandra.

"Well, I didn't know Dad wasn't here!" he said defensively. "I just wanted to talk to him."

Mom sighed. “No—” she began, but Sebastian didn’t let her finish.

“Okay if I go for a walk?” he interrupted. “Please?”

She stopped what she was trying to say and sighed again. “Yes. Go on. Take your phone. Home in an hour, please.”

Sebastian nodded and headed out of the office. He ignored Cassandra—who was standing in the living room doorway—as he let himself out of the house. This time, he turned toward the small strip mall in the other direction from the park. Sebastian walked fast, burning off his frustration.

It wasn’t fair. No one ever took him seriously!

He didn’t realize how far he’d gone until a quiet, stern voice nearby asked, “Something on your mind, son?”

Sebastian looked up to see the Major, an unhoused Army vet. He stayed in the small gardens on the other side of the strip mall’s parking lot. Everyone in the neighborhood knew the Major. He was always polite to others and enjoyed chatting with the schoolchildren when they stopped at the mall to buy snacks.

"Oh, hi, Major," Sebastian said. "Yes, I'm having a bad day."

"Oh dear." The Major patted the spot on the bench next to him. "Take a seat and tell me all about it."

Sebastian hesitated, but only for a moment. He was desperate to confide in someone. Dad was best, but the Major was also helpful. He sat and explained all of his problems to the man. Wanting to fit in with the other guys; not feeling able to say no to Cassandra and being teased about babysitting; those mean adults laughing at him; Dad not being home when he needed him; and Mom about to scold him. Sebastian talked for twenty minutes, barely taking a breath.

When he finally came to a stop, the Major drew in a deep breath of his own and shook his head. "Well!" he said. "That's quite a day you've had." Sebastian nodded miserably. "But are you sure it's truly that way?" The Major's voice was still gentle, but his words made Sebastian sit up and turn to face him sharply. "Maybe you need to change your perspective on it all."

"What do you mean?"

"Well, now." The Major rubbed his hands on his knees as he thought for a moment. "You didn't want to take Cassandra with you, but you still said yes to her, right?"

"Right."

"Then it's not fair of you to blame her for anything that happened after that, is it?" Sebastian opened his mouth to protest but then closed it again. The Major didn't wait for his reply anyway. "And you say your mom was mean to you, but it sounds more like she's worried about your dad. You just assumed she was going to scold you."

"But the boys didn't want to play ball with me!" Sebastian burst out. "They laughed!"

"Oh, Sebastian." The Major sighed. "I don't think the boys meant any harm. Is it possible it was just a little friendly teasing?"

"Maybe," he said stiffly and with a glum shrug of his shoulders. "But I still don't like it."

"I know," the Major said comfortingly. "But everyone goes through things like this at least once. You can choose to see everything from your own point of view all the time. But you'll always be disappointed if you do."

Sebastian thought for a moment. He didn't like the sound of that. He felt a pout forming on his face and tried to stop it.

"What's the alternative?" he asked eventually, hoping there was one.

The Major smiled, his face creasing into kindness. "To change," he said simply. "When something upsetting happens, *think* about it, think critically. That means going deep into the question. Why has that person done that thing? Are they being mean or just thoughtless? Are they upset about something that has nothing to do with you? And can you help them with it?"

"Oh." Sebastian thought about how his bad day could have gone differently. If he hadn't had Cassandra with him, he *might* have been invited to play the game. As he thought back over it, the laughing boys had been smiling with friendliness. They *hadn't* meant to be mean! Sebastian looked at the Major, his eyes widening as he realized this. But then . . . "But the Cuthbertsons *were* mean!" he added. "They called us names!"

The Major nodded. "Sure. Not everyone is nice.

But is that your problem or theirs?"

"Theirs?" Sebastian asked, not sure if it was the correct answer.

"Theirs." The Major nodded again. "And once you realize that, you won't get so upset by it."

Sebastian thought for a moment. He appreciated the way the Major explained everything. *I need to change,* he thought to himself. *I cause my own problems because I take things personally instead of understanding what's really going on.*

He looked up at the Major, ready to say thank you, but heard a harsh voice from behind them.

"Disgusting! Homeless vagabonds loitering everywhere. They're so dirty and smelly!"

Sebastian and the Major turned to see the Cuthbertsons strolling past. Their noses were in the air, and they had unpleasant expressions on their faces. They looked as if they smelled something rotten.

"It shouldn't be allowed!" Mr. Cuthbertson didn't turn his head, but Sebastian saw that he was trying to see if the Major was listening.

"I agree!" Mrs. Cuthbertson sneered. "We should

get our *lawyer*, Thomas Madison at BL, to do something about it!"

Sebastian stiffened with worry, but the Major didn't react. It was as if he couldn't hear the Cuthbertsons at all!

He smiled at Sebastian and said quietly, "Their problem. *Theirs!*"

Sebastian briefly smiled back at the Major. Despite the older man's brave words, there was sadness in his eyes. A thought occurred.

"Hey, Major? You're not at all what they said. But you don't own a shower or washing machine. How..." He hesitated, not sure if he was being rude. "How do you do those things, if I can ask?"

"I don't mind at all. Curiosity is a wonderful thing if handled right. Without it, we wouldn't know very much at all! I have some money along with my Army pension. It's enough to live on, and I have more than enough to pay for a membership at Smith's Gym." Sebastian frowned, confused. "I go to the gym every morning. I have a steam in the sauna, followed by a shower. Then I get a cup of coffee to set me up for the day. I have a locker there too, where I keep my clothes, and I change them daily. I use the laundromat across the road from there." He pointed down the street to Nan's Speedy Cleaners.

"Oh!" Sebastian was fascinated. He had never really thought about what it was like to not have a home. He accepted the Major as being just a part of his life. As he realized this, a warm flush reddened his face. He understood what the Major had been saying about critical thinking. "But don't you want to live in a house?" he asked.

"Not really," the Major said. "When I left the Army, my sweet Jennie was gone. I've got a photo, see?" He took out his old but well-polished leather wallet. He removed a small photograph showing a young, happy couple. Their arms were around each other as they laughed at the camera. Sebastian looked at it, focusing on the Major, who had a very impressive mustache and was wearing captain's stripes. They were standing under an ornamental arch that was decorated with balloons, white cardboard doves, and intertwined Js and Ss. "I couldn't bear to be alone in our home, where we'd been so happy. So I packed up the precious things, put them into storage, and handed the keys over to the landlord. Let a family live there and be happy, that's what I thought."

The missing woman Sebastian had seen on the television earlier came to his mind. He was about to say something when his phone buzzed as a text message came through. It was from Mom.

Where are you? One hour!!!

Sebastian checked the time and leaped to his feet. "I'm so sorry, Major. I'm late. I have to get home!"

He quickly typed: *Sorry! On my way now, five mins!*

"Off you go, lad." The Major was smiling sadly at the photo of his younger self and his wife. "You know where I am."

"Thank you!" Sebastian called as he started home. "I'll come back again soon."

The Major waved goodbye as Sebastian ran.

Chapter Three

Mom was making supper when Sebastian got home, and he immediately began to help by setting out the silverware and plates.

"Thanks, Seb!" Mom said, a bit surprised. She usually had to ask him to help out with chores.

"No problem," he replied. "I'm sorry I was late. I lost track of time. I was talking to the Major."

"Oh, you saw the Major, did you?" She smiled. She was fond of the tall, old soldier who reminded her of her grandfather.

"Yes." Sebastian moved around the table, setting the plates in the middle of the placemats. "He gave me some advice. I . . . I wasn't very nice to Cassandra earlier."

Mom gave him a look but didn't say anything. A moment later, the timer on the oven rang, and she turned to take out the pasta bake, asking Sebastian to shout for Cassandra to join them.

Mom added, "Dad's still not home. I'll be sure to save him a serving."

Feeling awkward, Sebastian apologized to Cassandra as they ate. "I'm sorry I was a jerk, Cassie," he said. "I shouldn't have taken it out on you."

Cassandra looked at him and nodded, agreeing with him, then turned back to her meal. He was confused. He had apologized! The least she could do was accept his apology! Then Sebastian seemed to hear the Major's quiet chuckle in his ear. He wanted Cassandra to accept his apology, he realized, so that he would feel better. But the point of apologizing was so that *she* would feel better. He looked at his sister.

"I won't do it again," he promised. "At least, I'll do my best not to."

Cassandra still didn't speak (her mouth was too full!), but this time, she smiled at him. He knew they were friends again.

After dinner, Mom cleaned the kitchen like she was angry with it, scrubbing the pots as though they had offended her. After putting Cassandra to bed, she joined Sebastian in the living room. He was watching the end credits of his favorite show. She sat tensely on the couch, looking away from the screen.

"Are you okay, Mom?" he asked hesitantly.

"I'm fine." Her reply was abrupt, and Sebastian felt hurt like she had snapped at him. He realized the pinched lines around her mouth and the way her eyebrows were pulled together weren't signs of being grumpy. She was worried. He tried to talk to her, thinking maybe she would appreciate being distracted from her worries, but it didn't work. Eventually, she sighed and shook her head.

"Go on, son, it's bedtime now."

"I want to wait until Dad gets home!" Sebastian protested.

"He probably won't be home tonight." Mom tried to sound calm, but her voice still had that worried edge to it. "Go on. Off to bed." When he hesitated for a moment, she added, *"Now."* There was no arguing with Mom when she used that voice.

Sebastian got to his feet with a sigh and stomped out of the room. While he was brushing his teeth, he remembered that he was trying to be more grown-up. And that meant being more thoughtful, which immediately made him feel bad.

"Night, Mom!" he called down the stairs, trying to convey that he was no longer sulking about being sent to bed.

"Night!" she called back, not letting on that she had noticed his moodiness.

When Sebastian got into bed, he thought about Mom and how obvious it was that she was worried. How often had he assumed that people were angry with him when they were thinking about something completely different? Did that make him a bad person? Was the neighborhood full of people who thought Sebastian was the most unaware person in the whole world?

Then another thought occurred. Was thinking this way just another kind of selfishness? He was worrying about what people thought about him instead of worrying about the people. *Oh, it's all so confusing,* he thought. It was hard being mature and sensible!

But his bed was warm, and he was pleasantly tired and well-fed. It wasn't too long before his thoughts were chased away by sleep. He dreamed of playing baseball, hitting the ball out of the park, and being cheered on by the Major, Mom, Dad, and even Cassandra.

At breakfast, Mom was pale with dark rings under her eyes.

"Are you sick, Mom?" Sebastian asked cautiously. "You don't look okay."

"I didn't sleep very well last night," she admitted. "I . . . I wish your Dad would come home."

"What's he doing, anyway?" Cassandra asked curiously as she spooned up her favorite cereal. "Is he on a case?"

"Yes." Mom sighed, pushing her toast around the plate but not eating it. "He's working for that lawyer who wants him to find someone."

"Do you think he's all right?" Sebastian asked the question tentatively, not sure he wanted the answer.

"I think so," she replied. "No news is good news. If he'd gotten into an accident or something, someone would have told us. I just wish . . ." She fell silent, watching as a blob of honey slipped off her toast and pooled on her plate.

After breakfast, Sebastian and Cassandra cleaned up. Mom settled down behind the computer in her room to start the work day.

"Hey, Cassie," Sebastian started. "How do you think we can find out where Dad is?"

"We can just use Find My Phone," she said with a shrug.

"I'm sure Mom's tried that already. But yeah, we can try it ourselves, I guess." He took out his phone and pressed the buttons that called up Dad's cell location. After buffering for a moment, the screen showed that Dad's phone was somewhere *in the house*. Frowning, Sebastian pressed the green phone icon to call him. He tilted his head, listening.

"I hear something!" he exclaimed. He moved toward the kitchen door and followed the sound to its source.

"It's coming from Dad's office," Cassandra said.

Sebastian hung up and the melody stopped. "You're right," he agreed, putting his phone away. "I've got an idea. Let's look around in Dad's office. Maybe we can work out what he's doing from the clues he's left."

"Like . . . *detect* where Dad's gone, you mean?" she asked.

"Exactly!"

They turned on the light in the office and looked around. The desk was as clean and tidy as it had been yesterday. Cassandra surveyed the space with her hands on her hips. Sebastian moved to Dad's shelf of file boxes, looking for the one labeled "open cases." Dad currently had three cases.

One case was about a missing dog. Dad had worked out that the man's ex-girlfriend had taken the dog. He just needed to find a way to get it back before closing the case. He'd made a note that the ex-girlfriend would be away from home one day next week, and he would retrieve the dog then.

Not that one, Sebastian thought. *Next*.

A man wanted to know what his business partner was spending all their profits on. Dad had scribbled "Vacation booked in the Caymans. Warn him." Sebastian puzzled over that one, not sure what it meant.

Next.

The third case concerned a woman whom a lawyer wanted to find. The lawyer hadn't been able to contact her for many years but needed her signature on some paperwork. Sebastian had difficulty understanding all the legal language in the file.

"Find anything?" he asked Cassandra hopefully, seeing she had climbed under the desk.

"Not sure. There's a bit of paper here, with . . . it looks like a zip code." She wriggled out, patches of gray dust on her knees, and handed him the scrap.

"Yeah, zip code," Sebastian agreed as he squinted at it. "Part of one, anyway. The first number's missing. Something, four, six, two, zero. Let's take this to my room. I'll carry the files and Dad's notebook and . . ."

"I'll bring this shoebox," Cassandra added, picking it up from where it was tucked under the desk. "It's got photos and stuff in it. It's not dusty at all, so I think he's used it recently. And this fat envelope too. It was in Dad's in-tray."

"Good idea," Sebastian said. "In fact, bring the whole in-tray."

OPEN
CASES
CASES

"Okey-dokey," Cassandra replied happily as she loaded up her arms and headed to the door. He followed, shuffling the file box and the notebook together.

Two hours later, they were stumped.

Something about the missing woman case told Sebastian that this was the one. He spent a moment imagining Dad, wearing a cowboy hat and riding a horse, tracking a woman across a desert. Then he shook his head, shooing away the thought. He didn't even know if Dad could ride a horse, there were no deserts around them, and there was no need for the woman to run away. He was just being imaginative.

When Cassandra unpacked the shoebox, there was a photograph of a woman with a sad, sweet face. A slip of paper was clipped to it, bearing the name of the lawyer who was looking for the woman. Sebastian deciphered the writing as saying, "This is her, though she is obviously much older now. Good luck! JM of BL."

"This is the woman Dad's looking for!" Sebastian exclaimed. He frowned. "I think I've seen her somewhere before."

"Really? Where?" Cassandra asked.

He thought for a moment. Something tickled his mind. Something about a *different* missing woman? He tried to think, but the feeling vanished. "Argh!" he exclaimed. "I wish there was a way to . . ." He waved his hands in frustration at the piles of papers and photos that were stacked all over his bedroom floor. ". . . organize all of this!"

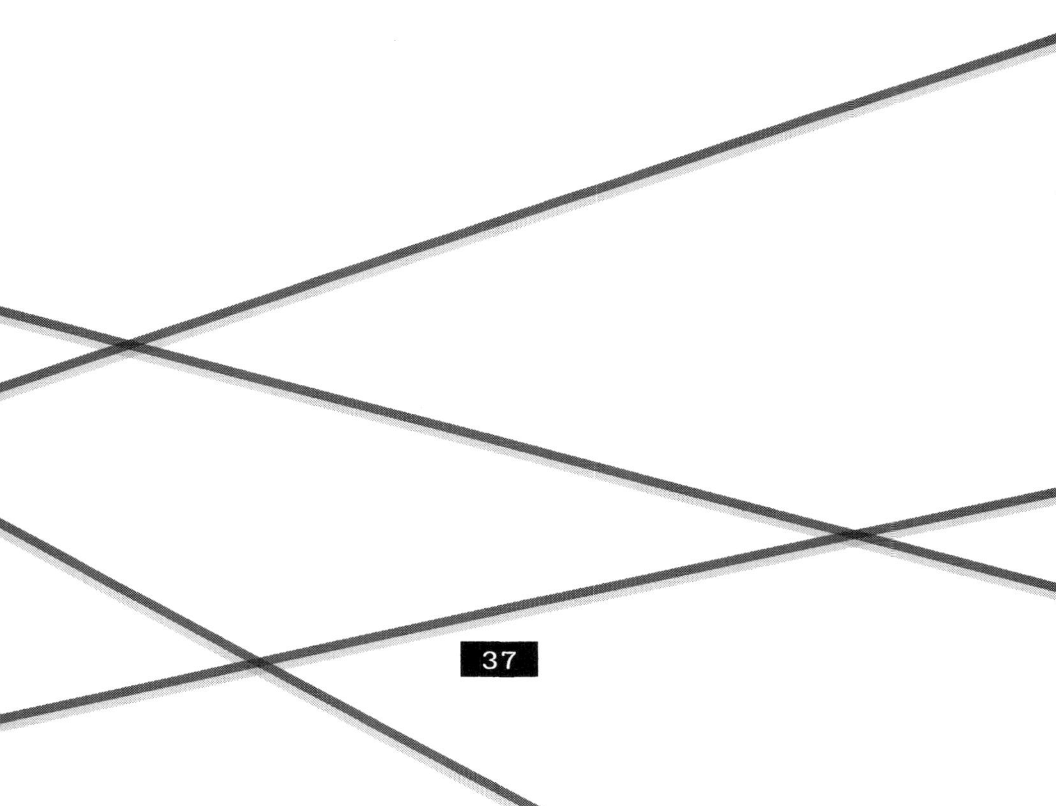

Chapter Four

"Ooh! I know a way!" Cassandra exclaimed. "Mom showed me! I was stuck writing one of my stories and it sure helped."

Cassandra loved writing adventure stories about a small cat that explored his neighborhood and learned all about the world. The stories were cute, but Sebastian's first thought was to dismiss such a silly idea. How could something meant for fiction help to solve a real-life problem?

Then he remembered that he was trying to be a better person. And also that he owed Cassandra for not staying upset with him when he had been mean to her the day before. *Besides,* he thought, *it might help.*

"Okay," he said. "How does it work?"

"When I'm stuck with a story," Cassandra began, "I write down all the steps of it from the beginning to where I got stuck. And then, I get a piece of paper and write down five things that could happen. Mom called it mind mapping."

Even though Sebastian couldn't see how it would help them find out what Dad was doing, he said, "Okay, where do we start?"

"Don't you remember?" Cassandra's face was glowing with excitement. "The other night? Dad was talking to Mom about the case, and he said it was a law firm in . . ." Her face scrunched up as she tried to remember what he had said. "I can't remember the name of the town, but we can find it out because Mom said—"

"Yes!" Sebastian suddenly recalled the conversation. Mom had made her delicious lasagna. Even though he had been very focused on finishing his serving so he could have seconds, he remembered the conversation at the table. Dad's new client was a lawyer from a town to the southwest.

Dad had said, *"I've never been there, I don't know how he heard of me, but he said I came highly recommended."* Dad had shrugged, laughing at how strange it was.

"Oh!" Mom had said. *"That's where Jemma Hutchinson's family moved to."*

"Ah!" Dad had replied.

Jemma Hutchinson was a little girl whose grandparents had kidnapped her, wanting her to permanently live with them. Dad had found them hiding in a trailer park and persuaded the grandparents to return Jemma to her mom and dad.

"Yes!" Cassandra said. "Mom put the article about the case up on the wall in Dad's office. She said so the other night. I'll go read it."

In a moment, she was back, panting from rushing down and up the stairs so fast. "Bostock Town!" She grinned.

"Great!" Sebastian's eyes widened as he remembered seeing a bunch of papers and photographs all stamped with the words, "Bostock Law: Fixing Legal Matters Since 1988." He shuffled through the paperwork from the large envelope and soon found what he was looking for. "Dad said something else." He stared into space as he tried to recall it. "Something about signing papers and not trusting new people." He shook his head, unable to remember the exact phrasing, just that he'd mentioned several names to Mom. He wished he hadn't been so focused on the lasagna!

Cassandra was still thinking about the lawyer. "What's so important about signing stuff?" She frowned.

Sebastian shuffled the legal papers to the front of the little sheaf and read through it. It was difficult to understand, and he felt frustrated. Then he remembered something his English teacher had said when the class was struggling to read a poem.

"Try reading it out loud. It can help make sense of the words," she had said.

Well, why not? Sebastian gave it a try. He ran his finger over the words, saying them quietly out loud. It worked! The long, complicated sentences began to make sense. He understood that the papers to be signed were to "settle an estate." To him, that sounded like someone was trying to calm down a house—but that didn't make sense. He quickly typed the phrase into a search engine on his cell phone. He saw that the word "estate" meant everything that someone left behind when they died: money, houses, all their clothes, books, and pictures.

"Oh! She has to sign so she can have all the dead person's things!"

"Ooh," Cassandra said, a little shocked but also interested. "I wonder if she's going to be a millionaire! Can you imagine?"

"Mmm." He barely acknowledged his sister as he was still scanning the letter. "It just says 'a considerable estate.' I don't know what that means exactly. Pretty big, I guess?" He read the last section. "Oh! If they can't find her, they'll look for some cousins who will then get everything."

"Oh." Cassandra made an annoyed face. "That's not fair! It belongs to the lady!"

"But if they can't find her . . ." He trailed off.

He wrote down everything they could remember Mom and Dad talking about over dinner the other night. They laid out all the clues that referred to the woman: the photos, the legal letters, newspaper clippings that all said something like, "Will Jeanette Smithson nee Du Pois please contact James Marvel at Bostock Law urgently." Either Dad or the lawyer had clipped them together. A sticky note was attached that had the scrawled words: "No result."

"They put advertisements in the newspapers," Sebastian said, tapping the clippings, "but they didn't get any replies."

Cassandra nodded, her eyes wide.

"I wonder why they didn't include a photograph of her?" He thought out loud. "That way, even if the woman—what's her name? Jeanette Smithson? Even if *she* didn't see it, someone else who knows her might have . . ."

"Good point." Cassandra was impressed. "Like the lady on the news yesterday—" She stopped short, perhaps remembering that had been a bad day. Sebastian glanced at her, then turned back to the pile of papers.

"Okay," he said. "So, we know Dad's client is from Bostock Law, probably, um . . . that lawyer, what's his name? James Marvel? And he's looking for a woman who's going to inherit a lot of stuff from . . . *someone*." He looked at the pile of clues but couldn't find the name of the person who had died listed. "That's everything we know for sure. What do we do next, with your mind mappy thing?"

"Um, work out what comes next. Let's come up with several possibilities. So, Dad would have . . ." Cassandra thought for a moment, "maybe . . . Googled the lady?"

Sebastian was doubtful. "That's too obvious, isn't it? The lawyer could have done that." Cassandra shrugged. "Although, we might as well try it. We'd look silly if we didn't, and there she was all along! It's your idea, want to do the search?"

Cassandra brightened up. She nodded happily and carefully took Sebastian's phone from him. She spent a moment making sure she spelled the name correctly. "What does 'nee' mean?" she asked.

"Oh, I know that! When people get married and change their name to their partner's, they use 'nee' to show what their old name used to be. It means 'born' in French."

"There are no results for that name either way," Cassandra said mournfully.

"Shoot." Sebastian took his phone back.

"Okay, so that's a dead-end." Cassandra shook her head, thinking. "So, for the mind map, let's think what might have happened to the lady. Maybe she moved out of state?"

"True," Sebastian said thoughtfully. "Or even out of the US! She might have married someone else."

Cassandra looked at him, horrified. "How will they ever find her if that happened? What if she *does* have a different name? It'd be impossible!"

He shook his head. "It's a bit harder, but not impossible. There'll be registers and things showing who she married and when she changed her name." He spoke confidently but wasn't sure how it all worked. "She might've died," he added.

"Oh, *that* would be sad," she muttered. "I hope it's not that."

"Me too," he agreed. "Or . . ." He fell silent, tugging on his lower lip as he tried to think where else the woman might have gone. He shuffled through the clues, hoping something would catch his eye. Then he wrote down all the possibilities they'd come up with:

Married again, new name.

Living somewhere else (another state, other country)

Dead (hope not)

He looked at Cassandra. "Did you say five possibilities?"

"Yup." She twisted her neck to see the list he'd written. "But I can't think. What else is there? Just . . . living her normal life?"

"Maybe," Sebastian said with a shrug. "Maybe she committed a crime and went into hiding. Maybe that's why no one can find her."

"Ooh, yeah!" Cassandra's excitement returned. "She might already be super rich because she stole a fancy diamond!" Then she paused. "But then we'll never be able to find her."

He smiled. "I don't think she committed a crime. I was being silly."

"Oh, okay." She smiled too.

The thought of crime reminded him of something Dad had written at the bottom of the legal letter about Jeanette Smithson. It took him a moment to find the note.

Dad had written "*Cousins*. Not to be ________. Caution!" Puzzling over the hard-to-read word, Sebastian thought it said "crusted" but then decided it must be "trusted" instead. That made more sense. But who were the cousins? Dad had scribbled these notes to himself. He didn't mean for anyone else to see them, so none of them made anything clear. Sebastian set the page off to the side and turned back to Cassandra and the task at hand.

"What next. . .?" he asked, looking at their list of possibilities. He added some words to it.

Committed a crime!
Just being normal?

Cassandra watched him write the words then spoke up. "Um . . . well, with my stories, I choose the one I like the most. Uh . . ."

"I guess," Sebastian thought hard, "we choose the option that's easiest to prove? So, like, how do we find out if someone died?"

"I don't know." She shrugged. "Ask her family?"

"I don't think so," he replied. "Because otherwise, the lawyer would have known that right away if she had family who knew."

"Of course." Cassandra made a displeased face, then looked down at the pile of clues with a fed-up expression. "This is boring. I thought Dad just . . ." She waved her hands in the air. ". . . knew stuff, like looked at a couple of things and just solved the case. What do we do next?"

The truth was that Sebastian didn't know. He shrugged helplessly.

"I'm going to go watch TV," she announced. "If that's okay?"

"Sure," he said. "I'll stick with it a bit longer." He glanced at the time on his cell phone and was shocked to see it was nearly lunchtime. "Actually, I'll come down with you. Mom'll be making lunch soon."

After a lunch of sandwiches and cookies with a glass of milk, Sebastian returned to his bedroom. He looked at all the piles on the floor. There were newspaper clippings, photographs, and letters, along with sticky notes and envelopes on which Dad had scribbled notes to himself. One of them said, "Madison marvel prtnr—beware." And Sebastian had no idea what that meant! There were other odds and ends too: a military pin, a pretty enamel brooch with a swirly letter and lots of

flowers on it, and a strange bunch of metal tools on a key ring. After a moment of thought, Sebastian decided the tools were a set of lockpicks, and he wondered why Dad had left them behind. But he couldn't work out the pin or brooch at all! Who did they belong to, he wondered, and why did Dad have them?

Chapter Five

SEBASTIAN SPENT the next half hour staring at the list that he had drawn up and slowly shuffling through the clues from Dad's office. The only interesting thing was a rough family tree that Dad had sketched on an old envelope. It showed Jeanette Du Pois in the middle at the bottom, and then the branches stretched out sideways and above her, one short line leading to the name Captain John Smithson, showing that she had married him. *No kids,* Sebastian thought.

He tried to make out the names of Jeanette's other relatives. There were so many of them, all with different last names. There were Du Pois, Jameson, Roberts, and Simmons alongside longer names written in cramped handwriting. Sebastian could barely make them out other than they started with an L. Or maybe it was a C. Frustrated, he stood and stretched.

Suddenly, he remembered the Major telling him to change his perspective. The Major had meant he should think about a problem from a different point of view. But literally changing his perspective might also help! Sebastian carefully piled all the clues, notebooks, and boxes onto the whiteboard he had been using to make notes. He went back down to Dad's office and spread everything out on the big desk, leaning the whiteboard against the wall.

Being in the room reminded him of the scrap of paper Cassandra had found. He plucked it out of the pile of notes and studied it thoughtfully. Something about it looked familiar. He leaned back in Dad's chair, his eyes closed, and thought hard.

His eyes shot open as he realized what it reminded him of. The law firm! He took out the legal papers and looked at the address printed at the top. He was right. The first digit was missing from the scrap of paper, but the next two were the same as the zip code for Bostock Law. Sebastian felt as though a big light had turned on in his head. What if the two zip codes were from the same area?

Managing a shaky breath, he took up his phone and

tapped the first digit in, then the numbers 4620 from the scrap. He added "zip code," then pressed enter. He watched with wide eyes as the screen filled with information about a neighborhood in Bostock Town.

One of the top links was a residential database, showing all the people who had lived in those houses for the last fifty years. Sebastian saw that some houses had only had one resident, while others had changed inhabitants once a year or so. Not sure what he was looking for, he skimmed over the names, hoping to see something useful.

"Whoa!" His finger slowed its scrolling. "No way!"

He tapped on the name he'd found and, yes, it was true. He picked up the letter from the law firm, rereading all the information about the inheritance and what would happen if the missing woman could not be found in time. Suddenly, the "Madison marvel" note made sense too.

"That's it!" Sebastian exclaimed. "I think I know what's going on!"

His eyes were wide as he thought through his idea. It all seemed to fit together. Had Dad also realized the same thing Sebastian had found? He puzzled over it for a while, then suddenly remembered that Cassandra had found the scrap of paper *under the desk*. Maybe Dad hadn't noticed it had gotten torn off and fluttered down there. Which meant it was likely he didn't know the name.

Old photos of pretty young women suddenly appeared in his mind.

"Are they photos of different ladies? Or could they be the same?"

Could the missing woman from the TV show be the same one Dad was looking for? He tried to remember the name and number that had shown under the photos, but he hadn't been paying that much attention. Idly, as he thought about it all, his eyes wandered over the brooch and the military pin, and another piece of the puzzle moved into place.

"Of course! Jeanette!" He jumped up from Dad's chair, too excited to remain sitting. "'J!' Is it possible?" He paced around the office and jumped when he turned and saw Mom standing in the doorway. She was smiling at him, despite the anxiety etched on her face.

"Here's where you're hiding out. You look so much like your dad when he's on the case," she said. "He was just like that the other day before those new neighbors came over to introduce themselves to us. The Cuthersons?"

"You mean the Cuthbertsons?" Sebastian asked. "They came here?"

"Yes?" Mom seemed surprised by the urgency in his voice. "They said they were visiting all their neighbors. I didn't care for them much, but I don't know why. They did seem very interested when I said your dad was a private investigator." Mom frowned a little as she remembered. "Mr. Cuthbertson made a funny comment, something about maybe employing Dad on a job. But he laughed like he was kidding. I didn't get it. Dad said he was too busy anyway and ducked out before they could meet each other. I don't think he even heard their names." Mom shook her head and rubbed her face with both hands. "Anyway, come on, it's dinnertime."

Sebastian was shocked. "Already?! I just had lunch!"

"No." Mom smiled again, this time looking genuinely amused. "That was five hours ago! You really are *just* like Dad!"

Sebastian stared at Mom, feeling his tummy rumbling. *It* had noticed the passage of time, even if he hadn't! "Wow!" he said. "Time does fly when you're busy. Maybe Dad's just really busy with the case."

Mom shrugged. "Maybe. He did tell me a long time ago that there might be times when he won't come home for as long as a week. He said not to do anything for at least four or five days. If he was on a case and his photo was suddenly everywhere, it might make things awkward for him."

"Oh. That must be hard for you, Mom."

"It is," she said as she hugged him tightly. "Come on, let's go eat." She kept one arm around him as they headed toward the kitchen. Sebastian didn't pull away as he might have before, moaning that she was embarrassing him. *Besides,* he thought, *Mom hugs were always nice.*

Because of their secret research, Sebastian and Cassandra avoided each other's eyes during dinner. After they ate, he helped Mom wash up and then went over everything he'd learned. There was just one more thing to find out. He looked through all the clues and read all the papers one more time. He was startled to realize that one of the lawyers' letters wasn't a single sheet of thick paper, but two thinner pieces stuck together

from being so tightly folded. The back page listed all the things that the missing woman would inherit, from jewelry, to stocks, to real estate. Sebastian's gaze fell on the name of the person who had passed away, and all the breath left his lungs in a whoosh. He thought he knew where Dad might be. He would go there first thing in the morning, he decided, after checking all the clues again and making sure his ideas still seemed amazing and clever.

Sebastian settled down to sleep, certain that he would lie awake for hours worrying about Dad. But he fell asleep right away and didn't have any dreams at all.

Chapter Six

Sebastian woke up and knew it was very early in the morning. The sky was washed with the palest pink and gold of sunrise, and the birds were singing loudly outside his bedroom window. He dressed quickly and ran to Dad's office. Everything was exactly as he had left it, and a quick glance out the window let him know that Dad's car still wasn't parked in the driveway. Then, he worked logically through the progression of thoughts that had led him to his belief about where Dad was. It still all seemed to make sense.

"He must be there," he muttered. "I'll go see."

He wrote a note to Mom, telling her where he was heading and what he thought was going on. He tucked it half under Dad's desk calendar, with the word "Mom" clearly visible. If he got back in good time, he could just get rid of it. But if he didn't come home tonight, Mom would certainly find it where he left it.

Sebastian was tempted to rush off right away, but he made himself eat breakfast first. He didn't know how long he would be gone, and it seemed sensible to start the day with a full tummy. As he ate, he thought about what he might need and scribbled a list.

Once he'd eaten, he got his small backpack and filled it with the listed items. He was about to leave when he heard a soft footstep behind him. It was Cassandra, her long curly hair in a wild tangle and her eyes still sleepily scrunched up.

“I thought you were Mom,” she said.

“No, just me. I’m . . . going out for a bit.”

Pushing her hands into her pajama pockets, she gave him a long look. It was somewhat spoiled by her squinting against the sunbeams spilling through the windows. Then she simply said, “Okay. Can I have a hug?”

“Sure!” Sebastian was surprised, but happy enough to give his little sister a hug. After a moment, she stepped away.

“See you later,” she said, rubbing her eyes.

At last, Sebastian set off, heading through the park this time, his humiliating memory of the attempt to join the ballgame more or less forgotten by now. Ahead, he saw the Cuthbertsons with a gallon of milk and ducked behind a tree until they were out of sight. He didn’t want them to see him.

His destination lay on the other side of the park, about two miles down a narrow, single-lane road. Excited, he began to jog as soon as he was on the path. Sooner than he had expected, The Lodge loomed up in front of him, peaceful and sleepy in the early morning.

It was a large house near the edge of the neighborhood, and as far as Sebastian knew, no one was living there at the moment. He had known it was empty for ages, but it was only last night that he had realized why. The owner of the home, whose name he recognized in Dad's papers, had died and left everything to Jeanette Smithson.

He hesitated for a moment, half-hidden behind a tree as he looked through the tall gates, trying to see all the way to the house. Movement caught his eye, and he ducked out of sight as two uniformed security guards walked past, turning their heads to scan all around.

"Gate clear," one of them said into his crackling radio and received a garbled squawk as a reply. They marched on, and soon, the crunching of their footsteps faded as they walked out of earshot.

Sebastian decided not to try the gates. They were made of metal and chained together. They would make a lot of noise if he even touched them. Instead, he walked silently away from the gate along the wall. It was the right decision. Almost immediately, he found a gnarled tree that grew close to the wall, its branches drooping right over to his side.

Looking at the tree, Sebastian could see that if he climbed the wall to reach *that* branch, and then climbed over and slipped down on *this* side, he would be inside the property. It worked. Only a few minutes later, he was sitting against the tree trunk, snugly hidden by the drooping leaves. He could see the security guards approaching the house. They went in and closed the door behind them, the *clunk* of it shutting carried across the still lawn. Sebastian checked the time and saw it was just after eight-thirty.

He decided to wait and watch for a while. He would feel stupid if he were caught so quickly. He pulled out the binoculars. The long strap caught on Dad's notebook and pulled it out of the backpack too. He focused on the windows. After a moment, he saw the men sitting at a large table in what seemed to be a kitchen. They were with a third security guard, who was pouring cups of what looked like coffee. Sebastian watched them drink and chat, seemingly in no hurry.

As the minutes dragged by, Sebastian picked up Dad's notebook and leafed through it. A list caught his eye.

12:00 a.m.—5:00 a.m.—no

5:30 a.m.—5:35 a.m.—2

6:30 a.m.—6:35 a.m.—2

7:00 a.m.—7:35 a.m.—1

8:00 a.m.—8:05 a.m.—1

8:30 a.m.—8:35 a.m.—2

9:00 a.m.—9:35 a.m.—2

10:00 a.m.—10:05 a.m.—1

Every half-hour, but either one or two (seemed random) until . . .

10:00 p.m.—10:05 p.m.—1

10:30 p.m.—10:35 p.m.—2

11:00 p.m.—11:05 p.m.—2

12:00 a.m.—12:05 a.m.—2

Sebastian puzzled over it for a moment. Something happened for five minutes every half-hour during the day. The door thudded again, and he peered through his leafy camouflage. A different pair of security guards walked in a big circle around the house before patrolling along the wall. He froze as they approached his hiding place, but they didn't spot him. Their voices drifted to him as they passed.

". . . nosy detective, pain in the butt. Better take him a coffee and something to eat."

"Yeah, and the old lady too, until *they* decide what they're going to do with her . . ."

Nosy detective? That must mean Dad, Sebastian thought, his brain fizzing with nervous excitement. He strained his ears, but he couldn't hear any more of their conversation.

They completed their circuit and returned to the house. Sebastian glanced at the time again and saw it was just past nine o'clock.

"Dad was watching the guards, and he timed the patrols!"

He felt very proud of himself: he had followed the clues and ended up at the same place as Dad. He turned back to the notebook, flipping through the pages more slowly. He was hoping to find something else that Dad had noted, something that would help him work out what to do next. The only thing that looked useful was a map showing The Lodge and the grounds. There was the front gate and the door the guards were using. Obviously, Sebastian couldn't go that way. He saw there was a side door that seemed to be unused—even the guards' patrols didn't go very close to it.

There was a rustle in the branches above. Suddenly, with a thud, a small body landed next to him, making him jump.

"Hi, Seb!" It was Cassandra. She had climbed over the wall the same way he had.

He managed to restrain himself from yelling out but with great difficulty. "*Argh!* Cassandra! What? How did you find me?"

She giggled. "I put a tracking tag in your pocket when I hugged you," she admitted. "I could see you were in a hurry to go, and I didn't want to make you wait. But I want to help you. So I tracked you. Good idea to climb over the wall, by the way."

He stared at her, annoyance and amusement fighting to win his emotions. Finally, amusement won, and he laughed, shaking his head. "You are impossible, you know that?"

"Yeah!" She grinned at him, then turned to look at the house through the leaves. She twisted her head to look at the map that Dad had drawn, still open on Sebastian's lap. "So, what's the plan?"

"You stay here," he said firmly. "While I go in there—" He pointed at the side door on the map. "—and find the missing woman and Dad." He quickly recounted to Cassandra what he'd heard the guards saying.

"So he's definitely here?" she asked. "And no, I'm not staying here by myself, waiting for you. I'm coming too."

Sebastian was about to argue but then changed his mind. "Okay," he said. "You can come with, but we have to be deadly quiet, and if I tell you to run, you run, all right?"

"But—" she started, but he silenced her by holding up a finger.

"If I get caught, like Dad did, you need to run home and get Mom to call the police, okay? Besides, if anything happened to you, I would never be able to forgive myself."

"Oh." Cassandra thought about it. "Okay, deal."

They shook on it, and suddenly excited, Sebastian rose to his feet. "Okay, let's see what the guards are doing, then get to that side door."

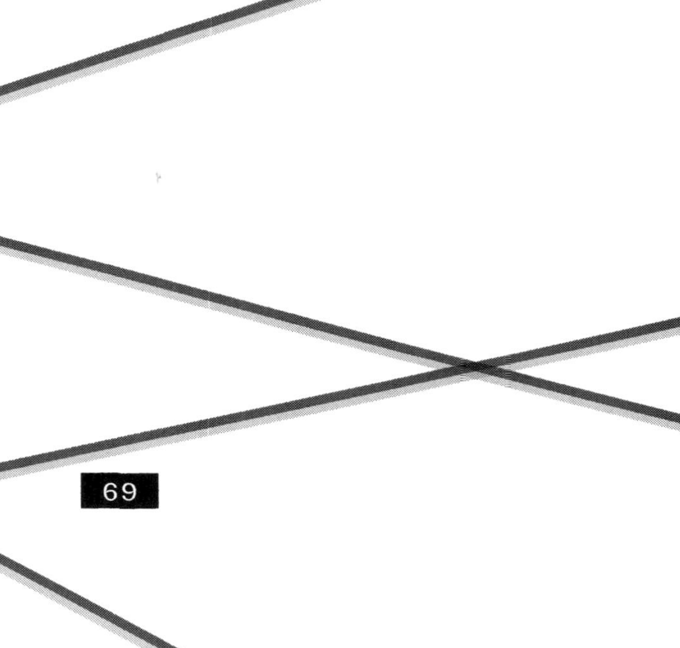

Chapter Seven

Peering through the binoculars, Sebastian could see the guards were all busy having breakfast—toast, cereal, and more coffee. He and Cassandra wasted no time, running as fast as they could to get around the corner of the house and quickly out of sight. He fumbled in his pocket for Dad's lockpicks as they approached the side door. He had only the vaguest idea of how to use them. But as they got closer, they could see that the door wasn't properly closed: it had been left so it looked shut, but the latch bolt hadn't entirely engaged with the frame.

"Dad must have done that," Sebastian whispered. "And he left it like this to be sure of getting out again."

"Smart!" Cassandra said, sticking to her brother's heels like a shadow. "And that makes it easy for us."

Sebastian turned the handle, holding tight so they didn't make a noise as the door eased open. Then, still holding the handle down, he pulled the door nearly closed again, not letting the latch bolt engage.

They tiptoed through the space, a disused dining room with a long, dusty table and twelve chairs arranged around it. They stopped at the door that led into the rest of the house. Voices came closer, and the kids silently panicked. They slithered under the table as quickly as they could. Just in time! The door opened and two pairs of legs—one clad in slacks, the other in a tweed skirt, and both wearing well-polished leather shoes—stopped in the doorway, where the kids had just been.

"He didn't come through here. No one's been here for months." The voice was female, harsh—and to Sebastian, instantly familiar. "All that dust."

"Yes." This voice was male. "The sooner we get the deeds and sell out to the developer, the sooner this dump will be gone. Good riddance too!"

"Good riddance indeed." The woman chuckled. "If only there was an easy way to get rid of our other little problem. Any ideas yet?"

"No." The man sounded grumpy about it. "And now we've got that nosy twerp down there too."

The man closed the door, but the handle didn't catch, and it rebounded open. But the pair didn't notice, as they were already halfway down the hall.

Under the table, Cassandra and Sebastian exchanged a glance. "Nosy twerp?" she whispered, her annoyance sparking despite her quiet tone. "Did they sound familiar to you?"

"Yes, it's the Cuthbertsons. What did they mean by *down there*?" Sebastian thought fast. "There must be a basement. That's where Dad and the woman are."

"Cuthbertsons!?" She seemed ready to run and yell at them for their evil ways, but instead, she nodded that he was probably right about the basement.

They got up and dusted themselves off as best they could. Cautiously, they set off in the direction the Cuthbertsons had gone. They were just approaching a stairwell when they heard footsteps coming up the stairs.

Sebastian reached over Cassandra's shoulder to the nearest door handle and backed her into the room

with him. To his relief, it was an empty bathroom. He pushed the door nearly shut and stood behind it, peeping through the gap in the hinge.

Two guards passed them, one carrying two empty plates and coffee mugs.

"Come on," the other said. "Time for patrol again."

Sebastian waited until the guards had gone into the kitchen, from where they would leave the house on patrol. Then, moving as fast as he dared, Sebastian led his sister down the stairs. As soon as they were out of sight, he slowed down, feeling his panicked heartbeat ease back to normal.

"Okay," he whispered, mainly to himself. "We should be fine now. We've got at least five minutes with only one guard in the house, plus they shouldn't be coming down here for hours."

She didn't reply, but she did squeeze his hand a little tighter.

At the bottom of the stairs, they turned right, exploring the long passageway as fast and as silently as they could. There were three rooms on this side, the doors all open and all of them empty. They each had a variety of broken furniture, old rolled-up carpets, and piles of boxes, most labeled with bold, black writing.

"Nothing!" Sebastian whispered. "Let's go check the other side of the corridor."

"Hello? Who's there?!" It was a loud male voice, sounding irritated and maybe a bit scared. But Cassandra and Sebastian recognized it immediately.

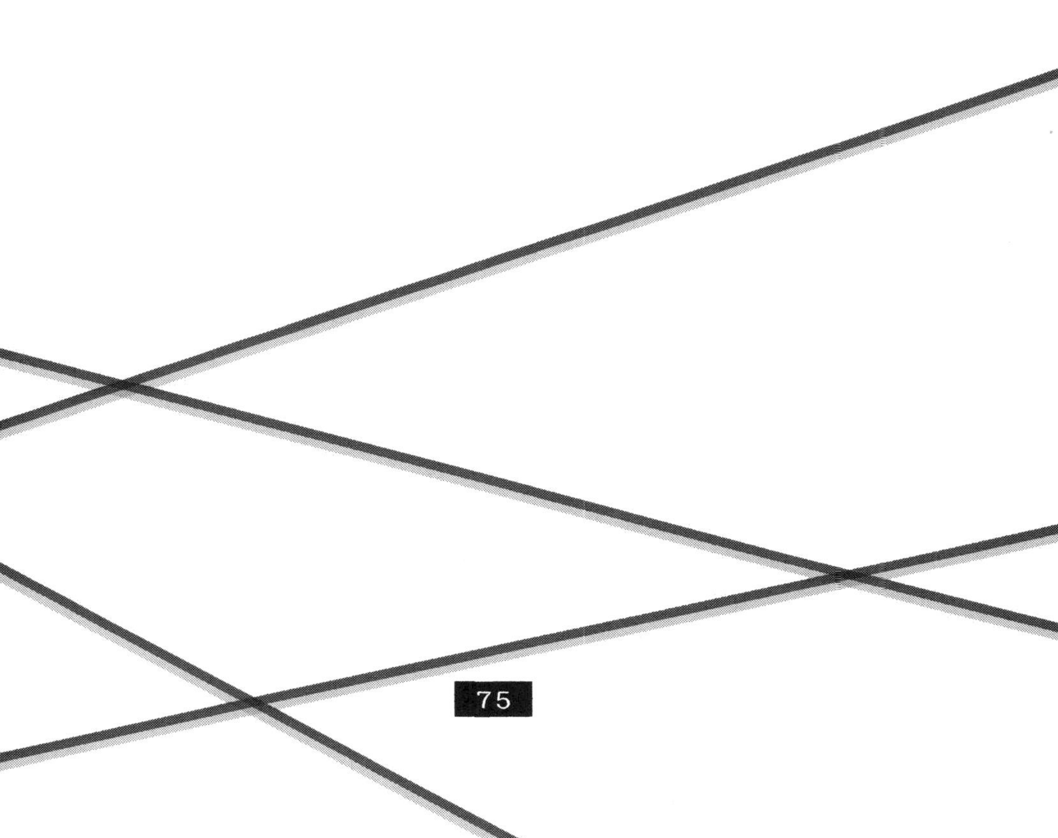

Chapter Eight

"Dad!" they called in unison, rushing forward to follow the voice. He was imprisoned in a small room with a sturdy cell door made of metal bars.

"Kids?!" Dad stared in amazement. "What are you doing here?"

"Finding you!" Sebastian said with a grin.

"Seb's very smart!" Cassandra added. "He looked at all the clues in your office and worked it out."

"That's great!" Dad was beaming with pride. "Great job."

"Cassie helped," Sebastian admitted. "She was great too."

Dad's grin widened even more, and he turned to the other person in the cell with him. "Jeanette? Ma'am?

These are my children I told you about." He turned to Sebastian and Cassandra.

The woman named Jeanette was a sweet, little old thing, and Sebastian recognized her from the photos he had seen. He smiled at her politely, but it was hard to keep his eyes off Dad.

"Nice to meet you," Cassandra said politely.

Dad turned to Sebastian. "Seb, can you find me a piece of wire or something to open this door?"

"I can do better than that." He grinned and pulled the lockpicks from his pocket. "How's this?"

"Incredible!" Dad exclaimed. He took the bunch of picks from Sebastian's hand and started to ease two of them inside the lock. "I'll have this open in a tick . . ."

It was just a moment until Dad swung the door open. But before any of them could move, they heard the scuff of shoes coming downstairs and voices echoing through the cellar.

The Cuthbertsons!

Sebastian and Dad had the same thought. "Inside!" they whispered.

Sebastian and Cassandra rushed into the cell with Jeanette and Dad. The kids flattened themselves against the wall so they couldn't be seen while Dad hurriedly put his lockpicks in his pocket and pulled the door shut again. Inspired, Sebastian stealthily reached for his own pocket.

Dad didn't wait for the Cuthbertsons to speak. "Who are you?" he demanded. "How dare you trap us here. Let us go immediately!"

Mr. Cuthbertson put his face close to the bars and stared at Dad. "You're an interfering fool!" he snapped. "But we knew you were looking for *her*, thanks to our lawyer, Thomas Madison. So we kept an eye out for you. And you crept right into our trap!"

"Madi—oh. James Marvel's partner at Bostock Law," Dad said as if he were realizing something.

Sebastian suddenly remembered the name under the woman's photo on the TV. It was James Marvel!

"But what do you want with her?" Dad added in a tone that was convincingly puzzled. "She's not harming anyone."

"Oh, but she is!" Mrs. Cuthbertson sneered. "She's standing in our way."

"Of what?"

Mrs. Cuthbertson rolled her eyes and spoke loudly. "She's between us and a great big fortune in our bank account, okay?"

"Yes," Mr. Cuthbertson agreed. "Our cousin, Petronius, should have left *us* all his money, but he didn't trust us for some reason . . ." He and Mrs. Cuthbertson took a moment to snicker at each other, clearly sharing a private joke. "So he left it to *her*, our mousy little cousin. Everyone thought she'd already died!" He pointed a long, bony finger at the woman, who flinched. "Well, we don't think that's very fair."

"Yes," Mrs. Cuthbertson added. "So we're taking matters into our own hands."

"That's illegal!" Dad said.

"So what?" Mr. Cuthbertson glared at him. "We've done plenty of illegal things!" They shared another maniacal laugh.

"What do you want?" Dad changed the subject abruptly. "Why are you down here?"

Mr. Cuthbertson looked around. "We thought we heard something." He shrugged. "Obviously just you, making a commotion as usual. Come along, my dear." He offered his arm to his wife, and they left, not looking back.

"Whew," Dad said as their voices vanished up the stairs. "Well, they've confessed, but I've got no proof of it. We need to get out of here, go to the police, and try and get them here before those two cut their losses and run. I don't even know their names!"

"Not necessarily." Sebastian grinned, holding up his phone to show Dad the screen. His recording app was still open, with one entry showing on the menu. "And *we* know their names, don't we, Cassie?"

"Yup." Cassandra grinned. "They're the Cuthbertsons."

"Oh!" Dad said. "They're one of my possibilities for the greedy cousins who moved into the area." His eyes sharpened on Sebastian's phone. "You didn't."

"I did!" Sebastian pressed play, and they heard Dad's voice asking, "Who are you?"

"*You did!* You absolute genius!" Dad pulled Sebastian into a big hug. "Can I borrow your phone?"

"Of course!" He handed it over and went to sit

next to Jeanette on the narrow bed as Dad dialed the police. "Hello," Sebastian said politely.

"Oh, hello, young man." She smiled at him. "I'm delighted to meet you. Your dad is very proud of you, you know."

"He is?" Sebastian felt a warm glow of pride. "I'm pretty proud of him too. Um, can I ask you a personal question?"

"Yes, of course." She sounded surprised.

"Do you have a nickname?"

She smiled sweetly. "My lovely husband's favorite book when he was a boy was *Jennie* by Paul Gallico. He used to call me that." Sebastian nodded, trying to hide his excitement. Momentary sadness flickered across her face. "He was an Army captain when I lost him."

"A captain!" Sebastian was now sure that he was completely right. He thought for a moment. "Could I ask what you mean, exactly, by lost him?"

"I mean he died, dear!" She sounded upset. "I got a message saying he was missing in action. They never found him. I knew that meant he'd died, and they didn't find—"

Dad had finished his phone call and moved over to listen to their conversation.

"Sebastian, don't upset Jeanette—"

"Dad," Sebastian started. "There's a photo of the Major somewhere in my phone. Please find it and show it to, um, Mrs. Smithson."

Dad looked startled but flicked through Sebastian's photos. "Here," Dad said, holding out the phone to Jeanette, showing the photo of the Major.

"Oh!" she exclaimed. "Is it possible? My beloved John! He's alive?"

"Yes!" Sebastian said. "You were gone when he returned, so he thought something had happened to *you*. He's here, in this town, living on the street." He took the military pin and the brooch from his pocket and showed them to her. Her eyes widened and she looked from one to the other, staring from Dad to Sebastian to the photo on the phone screen.

"Those were ours!" Jeanette clutched the phone tightly. "Alive. He's alive! Please take me to him!"

"Of course," Dad said, still looking at Sebastian with immense pride. "We'll take you there as soon as they—" He pointed up at the ceiling. "—are taken care of. The police are on their way."

When sirens sounded, Dad decided it was safe to go upstairs.

They ventured out into a comical scene. The three security guards were running away over the grass, dodging police officers who were chasing them, holding their handcuffs ready. Finally, one guard tripped, and an officer pounced on him. The other two guards got so distracted watching what was happening that they were soon caught and handcuffed.

Protesting that they were just doing their jobs, the guards were bundled into a police car and driven away. The Cuthbertsons were a different story. Mrs. Cuthbertson tried to scratch the detective's face and was immediately arrested.

Mr. Cuthbertson asked, "What's going on here?" pretending that nothing was wrong. When the detective began to read him his rights, he saw Jeanette standing by the door and tried to run away but was tackled to the ground in a moment. He was also placed under arrest.

The police spoke to Dad for a few minutes, got him to email them a copy of the recording, and then drove off, carrying the Cuthbertsons away from their dreams of ill-gotten riches.

As the police car moved down the long driveway, the Cuthbertsons glared at Sebastian and Cassandra through the back window.

The siblings high-fived one another behind Dad's back, with big grins on their faces.

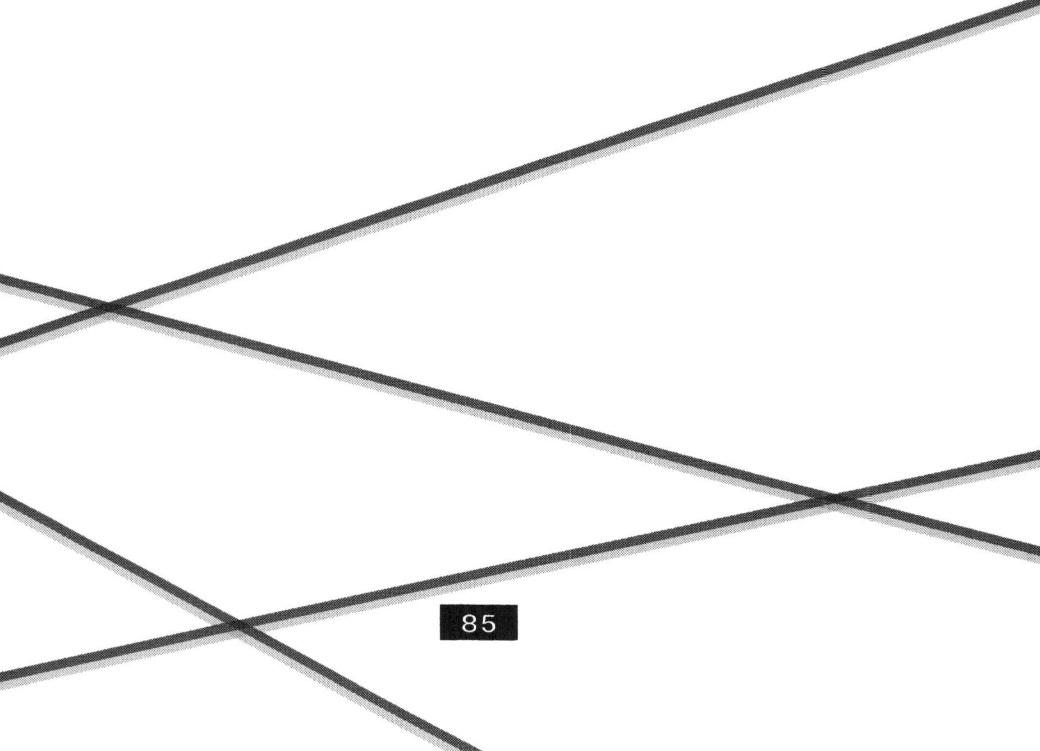

Chapter Nine

Sebastian spotted the Major first. "Let me go?" he asked Dad, who parked the car. "I'll give him a heads-up."

"Yes, good idea," Dad said. "Is that okay, Jeanette?"

She was looking at the Major, one hand pressed to her mouth, tears of joy running down her face. "Oh, yes, yes," she said. "I must fix my face! These silly tears."

"You look wonderful," Dad said reassuringly.

Sebastian didn't hear any more, as he was already on the way to greet the Major.

"Hello, son." The Major smiled at him. "I see you found your dad."

"Yes," Sebastian replied. "But we found someone else too."

He explained the case that Dad had been working on, and as he gave the Major the details, the older man sat up straight, his eyes wide and fascinated. When Sebastian got to the part where he and Cassandra had rescued Dad and the old woman, he couldn't contain himself any longer.

"The woman!" he exclaimed. "Is she truly Jeanette? Can it be . . ." His voice trailed off as Jeanette approached them, her face full of hope and love.

"John?" she asked.

"Jennie? Oh, Jennie!" He stood and swept her into his arms, hugging her closely, both of them murmuring to each other.

Sebastian watched them for a moment. He then began to feel uncomfortable and retreated to the car. Dad and Cassandra were watching the reunion from afar, happy tears in both of their eyes.

A little later, the Major beckoned them to join him. As they made their way over, Mom arrived, having been called by Dad using Sebastian's phone. They all went into a nearby restaurant, and Dad ordered the biggest burgers on the menu.

But the Major and Jennie seemed hardly aware of what they were eating.

"I love this town," the Major said. "We could live in The Lodge if it doesn't have too many bad memories."

"Yes," Jeanette replied. "I would live anywhere as long as you are there. There's so much space at the estate. We could do good things. Help the homeless, maybe?"

"Or an animal sanctuary?" the Major suggested, his eyes watching a stray cat cleaning itself in a sunbeam. He loved all the animals in the area.

"Anything you like!"

Dad grinned at everyone. "The papers are ready to sign tomorrow, villains are safely locked up, and there's a watertight case to keep them there. Let's do something else to celebrate this afternoon! My treat!"

"Oh, no!" Sebastian cried out.

"What's up, Rookie Detective?" Dad asked, still grinning. "You can choose: bowling or ice skating?"

"Both are good," Sebastian said. "But there's a pick-up baseball game happening today, and I want to play."

"We'll watch baseball," the Major volunteered.

"Me too," Mom said, smiling.

"Okay!" Dad changed his plans on the fly. "We'll all go watch Seb play ball. How's that?"

"Deal!" Sebastian grinned. He was aware that he wasn't even worried he might not be picked. He knew that this time everything would be all right.

And so it was. He was picked for a team and asked to hit second.

The first batter was up. He whacked the ball down the field and ran, making it to second base.

Sebastian readied himself, his eyes on the pitcher.

"Go, Seb!" Cassandra yelled from the side, making him smile.

The ball flew toward him, and his bat made perfect contact.

THWACK!

The ball flew down the field, bounced, and spun off in a different direction, the fielders who were chasing it fumbling all over the place. Sebastian ran *hard*.

First base.

Second base.

Third. He heard the crowd cheering the first batter home.

Mom, Dad, Cassandra, the Major, and Jeanette were all on their feet cheering and waving. Sebastian felt happy enough to burst from sheer joy. Could he get a home run?

Could he?

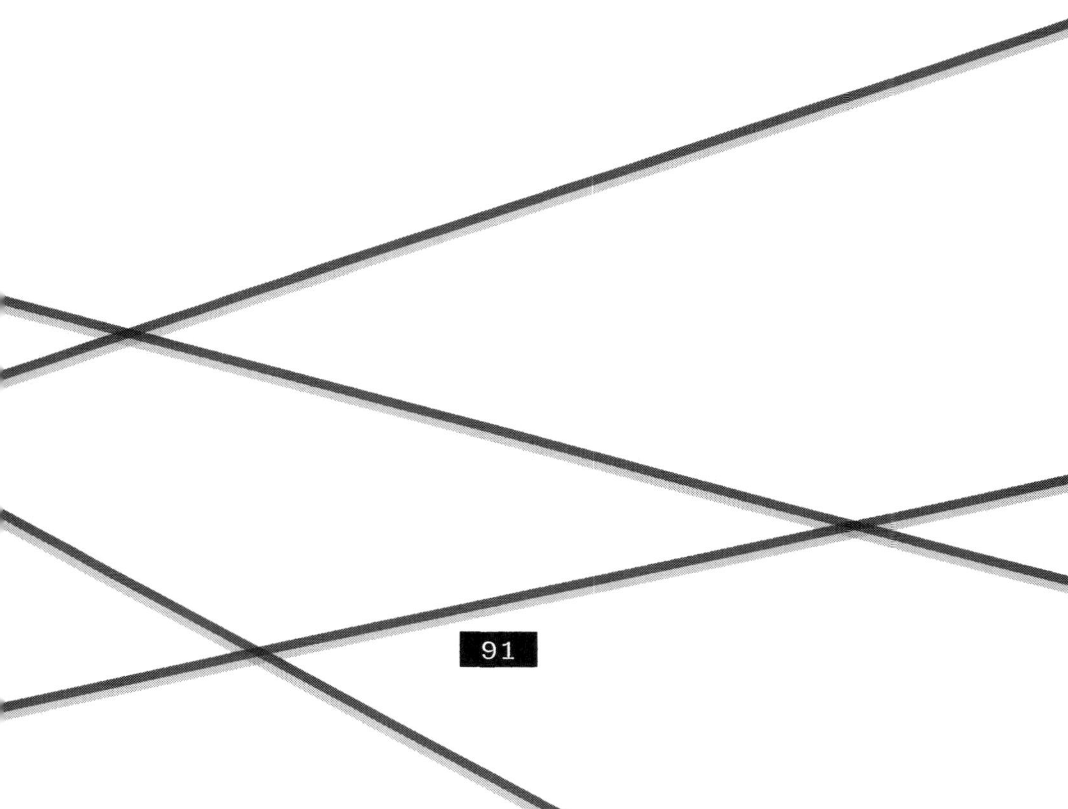

Each book that we have published has **a free audio version available.** To download the audiobook for *Rookie Detective*, **all you have to do is scan the QR code** or visit: www.littlebigpage.com/rookie

Made in the USA
Las Vegas, NV
08 December 2024